T0144984

A little BOOK of BIG things

Becky Forbes

Balboa Press books may be ordered through booksellers or by contacting:

Balboa Press
A Division of Hay House
1663 Liberty Drive
Bloomington, IN 47403
www.balboapress.com
1 (877) 407-4847

ISBN: 978-1-9822-2093-8 (sc)
ISBN: 978-1-9822-2092-1 (e)

Library of Congress Control Number: 2019901062

Print information available on the last page.

Balboa Press rev. date: 02/01/2019

BALBOA
PRESS
A DIVISION OF HAY HOUSE

A Little

Book

of Big

Things

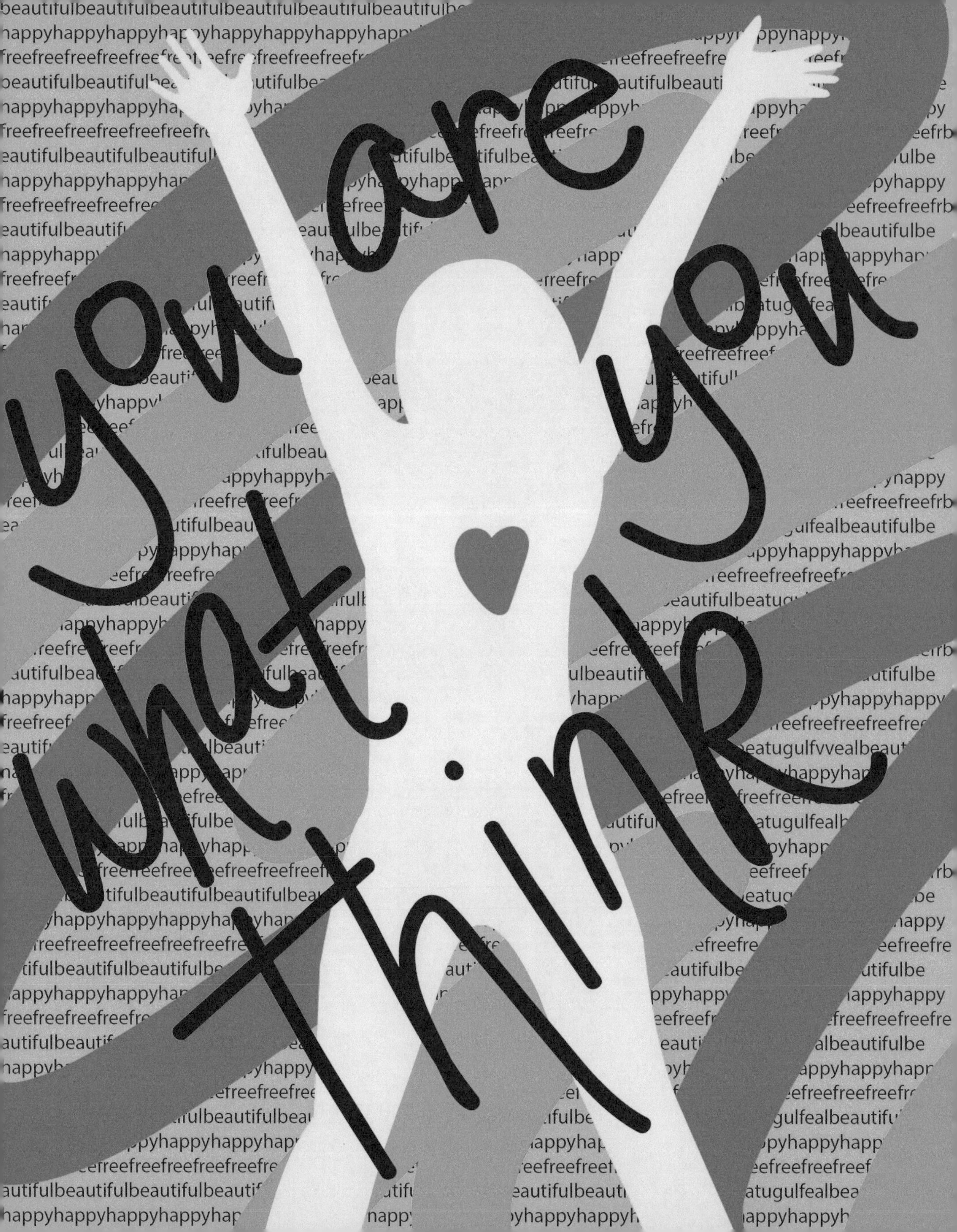
you are what you think

A girl, without even knowing it,
picked up beliefs along her way.
Her beliefs were her practiced thoughts.

- Hard work, long hours and pain are the road to success.
- All people are fake.
- She can never have what she wants.
- She can never rely on herself; only others can take proper care of her.
- She is not worthy of love.

She could only perceive the
world through her beliefs.

- She worked jobs that were hard with long hours.
- She trusted no one.
- She found people that wanted to take care of her, and
- She hated herself.

Life is a Stage

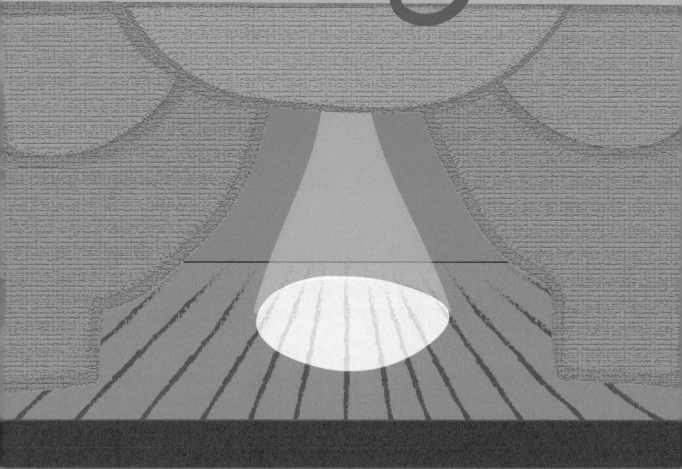

What's your Script

Her beliefs were constantly reinforced,
for they were all she could see.

Doubt, fear, and worry filled her thoughts.
Her days were dark, bleak and scary.
She felt death would be easier than life.

She did not know the stories she told
herself were only her perception.

AND THEY WERE NOT TRUE!

She did not understand that they
were of her own creation.
She thought they were real,
And she blamed her troubles on others,
For in her perception they taught her the beliefs.

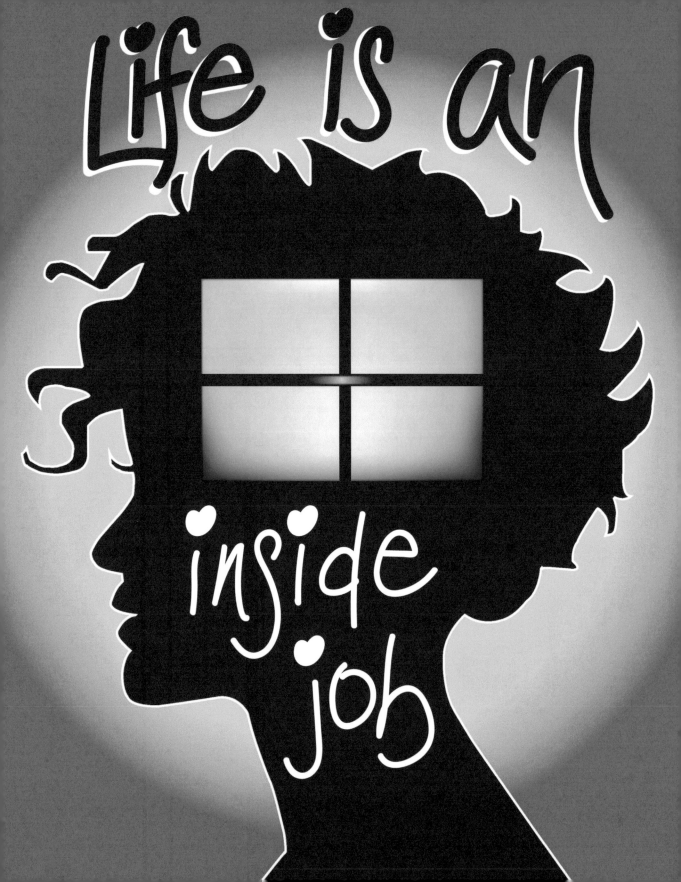

Yet, she yearned to be happy and free.

And through a series of events and discoveries she began the inward journey.

She learned that reality is her perception.

Perception is the story she tells herself.

The story she tells is her belief.

Her belief is her habit of thought.

HER REALITY IS HER
HABIT OF THOUGHT!

This discovery brought an Epiphany –

SHE CONTROLS HER REALITY
THROUGH HER THOUGHTS!

Every thought has two sides
- WANTED & UNWANTED -
HAPPY --- SAD
FREEDOM --- BONDAGE

The focus of her thought
creates her experience of reality.

She experiences what she thinks.

She can't be happy by thinking
about being sad.
She can't be free ruminating over bondage.

To rid herself of unwanted thoughts
She focuses gently on her desire;
And pretends she already has it.
(Or she distracts herself
and doesn't think about it at all.)

And she waits for inspiration to act.

to ~~Solve~~ Keep a ProBlem think about it

When the unwanted thoughts sneak
back in her mind, she doesn't worry.
She refocuses gently and
pretends again.

Pushing against the unwanted
thoughts only makes them stronger ---
She replaces them instead.

Many thoughts are so habitual
(BELIEFS are just thought habits)
that this process takes a while for her.

She is patient with herself.

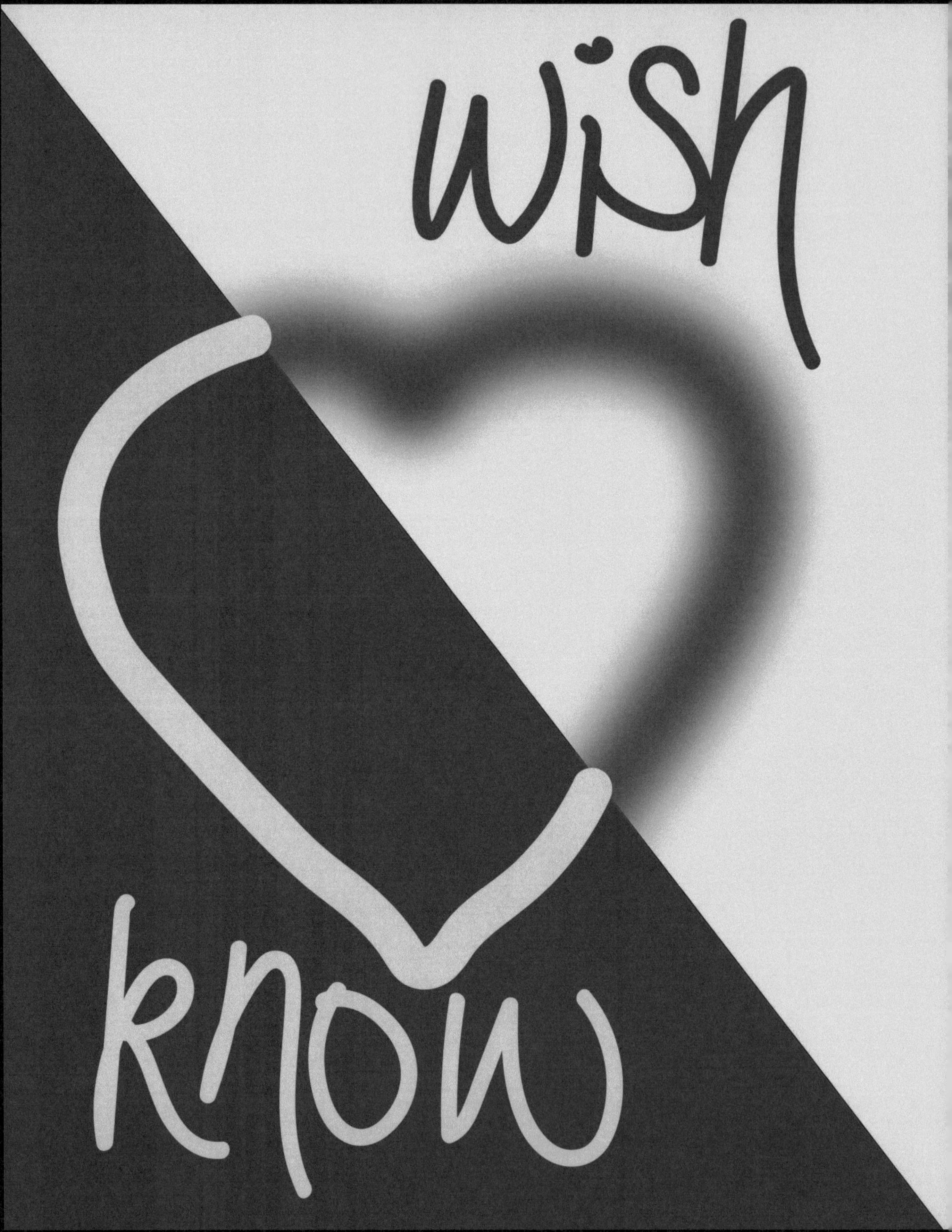
wish
know

Before she knows it, with gentle determination,
The pretending turns to KNOWING.

Once known, a thing comes to be.

And the inspiration flows.

She yearns to be HAPPY.

After she pretends for a time,
HAPPY comes to be her choice.

Every moment of every day.
She gets to choose.

She yearns to be FREE.

So she lets go of everyone
and
Allows them to be FREE.

SHE FOCUSES ONLY ON HERSELF,
And pretends she is FREE
until she KNOWS.

Every moment of every day.
She gets to choose.

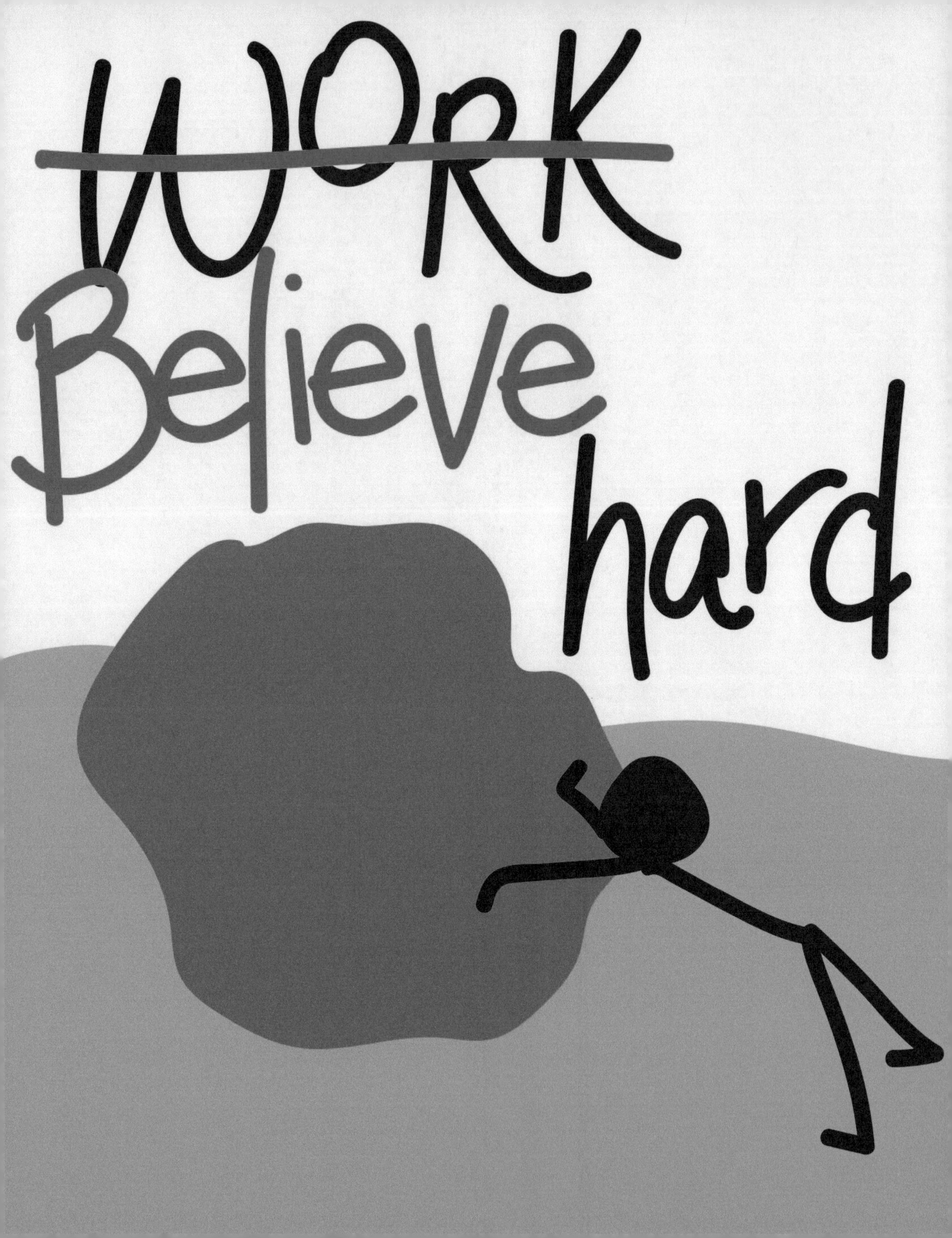
~~WORK~~
Believe
hard

She gives herself permission to

BELIEVE IN HER WORTHINESS.

She starts by pretending
until she KNOWS.

Every moment of every day.
She gets to choose.

She gives herself permission to

LET GO OF DOUBT.

She starts by pretending
Until She KNOWS.

Every moment of every day.
She gets to choose.

chill out

She gives herself permission to

RELAX.

She starts by pretending
until she KNOWS.

Every moment of every day.
She gets to choose.

the thoughts

you feed grow

She rests in her new-found
KNOWING.

And in her freedom Of choice
every moment of every day.

We are all
drops
of eternity

Life continues to reveal her
thought habits (aka beliefs)
by delivering unwanted experience.
(She knows it's unwanted 'cuz
it doesn't feel good.)

Each unwanted experience
brings the "want" into focus,
AND SO IT CONTINUES...
bringing endless opportunities to
pretend her way to knowing...
CREATING HER NEW REALITY.

Life Responds to you...
What do you want it to say..?

– It never ends –